Making Chocolates From Home

Tips and Tricks To Make Your Homemade Chocolates

Nick Ryan

Table of Contents

Making Chocolates From Home:
Tips and Tricks To Make Your
Homemamde Chocolates
By Nick Ryan

CHAPTER 1

Why Should You Make Homemade Chocolate?

There are people out there who always find it challenging to make their homemade chocolate, they get their chocolate cookies/chocolate bars at the store, and they never think twice about it. *But do you know that there lots of people out there who have been making homemade chocolate for over 100 years now?* Some believed that homemade chocolate tastes better than the commercial chocolate. Now tell me, who doesn't love getting a special treat that was made for them?

It's actually suitable for people who have dietary challenges (which makes it unhealthy for them to eat commercial chocolate packed with fat and sugar) to enjoy eating some chocolate without worrying much about the health issues they would probably face from eating the commercial chocolate.

People who have severe allergies to things mostly found in commercial chocolate, like nuts, have to be attentive about the brands and types of commercial chocolate they eat. Lots of people prefer to make this homemade chocolate because it's free from any nuts products.

Chocolate can cause havoc with a diabetic's blood sugar levels, which is a considerable concern for diabetic people. Doctors suggest that people who have Diabetes should eat only sugar-free chocolate or maybe give up chocolate. As far as it can be so challenging to get sugar-free chocolate, it's also not expensive but tasty. Making homemade sugar-free chocolate is an excellent option for people with Diabetes. *Do you have a diabetic person who is very close to you?* You can make him/her feel great at home, at the parties, or holidays by making special homemade sugar-free chocolate for them.

Another reason is that it's always fun when you make homemade chocolate at home. If you love cooking, you would probably enjoy the incredible process of deciding what kind of chocolates to make, the ways of making the chocolate, and the fun when eating the chocolate. Keeping your kids busy with this homemade chocolate would be great. Make these chocolates with them and share as gifts at a party, birthdays, valentines, Christmas, special holidays, and other beautiful occasions.

These are great gifts that people will really love. You don't have to spend a fortune making these personalized and unique homemade chocolates. Make yours today, and it's undoubtedly going to be a hit!

CHAPTER 2

Traditional Chocolate Making

Do you know that it's possible to make your chocolate the *traditional way?* Yes, it's possible, but it involves a lengthy process. It's vital to you to make all of your chocolate from scratch if you want to pursue making it as a hobby, but you'll be needing a lot of time on your hands and some specialized equipment.

You should give traditional chocolate a try because most people enjoy making chocolate from scratch, so you can see if it's a hobby you have an interest in. Below are several process and steps in making your traditional Chocolate:

1. **Choosing the Beans:**
You need some high-quality cocoa beans when you first start making chocolate the traditional way. The reason is that chocolate is made from cocoa beans, and if you need whole cocoa beans, it isn't too hard to get at all. Some suppliers offer different varieties of cocoa beans on the web. They offer them in different price ranges - you just have to go for the best!

2. Roasting the Beans:

We do roast coffee beans, right? So our Cocoa beans need to be roasted as well. Roast them in the oven if you want or buy a specialized cocoa bean roaster if you're going to pursue making traditional chocolate as a hobby. The beans take about five minutes or as more as 40 minutes, depending on the flavor you want or the kind of bean used.

3. Getting the chocolate out:

There are several ways to do this at home. The first thing you need is to crack and open the bean's outer shell to get the inside's chocolate - do this after the beans are roasted. Also, in a single sheet on a baking sheet, lay the beans and crack the shells using a hammer, open, then use a dryer to blow the beans' hulls away from the chocolate - do this on a low setting. You can as well use a juicer to achieve the same goal. This step is a little bit messy, so make sure you have a bucket and mop or any other clean up supplies with you.

4. Grinding and refining the Chocolate:

Many professional chocolate makers recommend using a high-quality juicer to grind your chocolate down as far as possible. You need to add sugar, milk, preservatives, or anything else to the chocolate to enhance the flavor - do this after grinding finely. Now the chocolate will need to agitate slowly but continuously as soon as you mix the ingredients. This process would take about 12 hours to get the chocolate to the right consistency. Professionals recommend doing this on a low setting using a stand mixer to refine the chocolate.

5. Tempering the Chocolate:

Your chocolates need to be tempered once they have been thoroughly refined. Tempering them can be a very stressful and complicated process, but you can use a microwave to increase the procedure a little. This way, your chocolate will be tempered. Your chocolate can be ready to eat or use when it's smooth, shiny, and hard.

CHAPTER 3

Making Amazing Homemade Chocolate Without A Lot of Work

The process of making chocolate traditionally might be a lot of hard work that you won't like. Some people love the long process of making chocolate traditionally, while some want it easier and faster to get their homemade chocolate ready. Well, the fun part of making this homemade chocolate is adding the flavor and using unique molds.

Use special chocolate wafers and chips that are made for candy making and skip the traditional chocolate-making process. This process will make it easier to get to the fun part of this homemade chocolate making. These wafers and chips are great because you can meltdown in a microwave or double boiler; they would make you have a tremendous smooth chocolate base to start with and be creative to decide what to add to the chocolate.

You'll be amazed at how creative you are when you use these wafers, chips, and bricks of this chocolate. It's far time consuming and difficult for most people to make the chocolate traditionally. They just want to make cool treats in their kitchen, they don't need lots of research or special ingredients, and they do not need to invest in lots of expensive equipment. All they want is to make their chocolate at home.

And if you're among these people that want to have fun when making chocolate at home, you should definitely get some chocolate base from a craft store or a candy supply shop and start to make your candy using those melted chocolates.

The melted chocolates are a great way to try out different chocolate flavors. If you want to add more special spices to your chocolate, you can get some very exotic chocolate bases that would cost a fortune. If you can also get the low fat and sugar-free chocolate bases, that would be great! It will decrease the need for you to buy the expensive ingredients that you'll be using.

Save some money and satisfy your families and friends today with amazing homemade chocolate. They would love it and feel great with the melt chocolate bases. I think they should appreciate you for this.

CHAPTER 4

Types of Chocolates to Use in Homemade Chocolate

There are lots of chocolates you can use when it comes to making your homemade chocolate, which depends on your tastes, and who you're making the chocolate for. For example, you should use dark chocolate to make chocolate for someone lactose intolerant or vegan because it doesn't contain any milk.

Below includes a quick overview of the most common chocolates you can use to make your homemade chocolate at home:

1)   Unsweetened Chocolate:
This kind of chocolate is mostly used in baking to add a rich flavor to food. You can use sugar-free chocolate and use something other than sugar to give it a sweeter taste. Most diabetic or people who are watching their sugar intake use this unsweetened chocolate and a sugar substitute to make their homemade chocolate taste good!

2) Dark Chocolate:

As previously stated, dark chocolate does not have milk in it, but it's great to use as a base for those that choose not to eat milk products. Some people enjoy the slightly bitter taste of the dark chocolate and the dark color.

3) Bittersweet Chocolate:

Bittersweet Chocolate has just a little sugar, but it's slightly sweeter than the unsweetened chocolate. You should go for this kind of chocolate if you don't want to use a commercial sugar substitute because it has less sugar than other chocolates. You can use this as a base of your homemade chocolate.

4) Semisweet Chocolate:

Semisweet Chocolate is one of the most popular types of chocolates used often in making chocolate chip cookies and candy. It's slightly sweeter than the bittersweet chocolate, and the sugar in this chocolate isn't too high and too low.

5) Milk Chocolate:

Milk chocolate is made with evaporated or condensed milk. It contains at least 12% of milk and a high level of sugar. It also has a shallow cocoa content that is very sweet and doesn't have the harsh or bitter taste that other chocolates have.

6) White Chocolate:

Most people believe this chocolate isn't part of the kinds of chocolates we have, but we just have to include it because it contains cocoa butter, milk, and sugar that is often flavored with any flavors whatsoever.

You can always try different flavors by matching and mixing these types of chocolates. For example, little milk chocolate would probably give your semisweet homemade chocolate a little bit richness to enhance the flavor. You can just play around with the chocolates listed here until you find a mixture that tastes great and makes that your desired chocolate base.

CHAPTER 5

Five (5) Tools You Will Need to Make Homemade Chocolate

Some books and magazines about candy making will say that you need to have a lot of special equipment to make chocolate at home, but that's not necessarily true. You need to have only five tools to make incredible chocolate at home, and you probably already have at least some of them in your kitchen. *The tools include:*

1. **Candy thermometer :**
Some chocolate candy needs to be heated to a specific temperature to be safe to eat. Some types of chocolate need to be heated to a particular temperature to be liquid enough to pour and set appropriately in a mold. It's also a great idea to have at least one candy thermometer on hand.

2.   Mixing bowls :

You will go through mixing bowls like crazy when making chocolate, especially if you combine other ingredients into a chocolate base. To save money on mixing bowls, go to your local Goodwill or Salvation Army store. Charity shops like that usually have kitchen and housewares sections where you can find great deals on glass and stainless steel mixing bowls. You can also look for mixing bowls at garage and yard sales.

3.   Pots and pans :

If you are using a pre-made chocolate base, you can heat that base in a microwave until it's liquid enough to work with, but you will need saucepans to mix other ingredients to the chocolate to the correct temperature. Like mixing bowls, you can often find mismatched pots and pans at charity stores and garage sales. When the chocolate recipe calls for you to use a double boiler, you can use two pans.

4.   Molds :

Once you have your chocolate blended just the way you want it and have added any extras that you want to add into the chocolate, you're going to need something to pour that chocolate into so that you can make chocolate candies. Having a wide variety of chocolate molds that are clean and ready to go is always a great idea.

5.   Candy Coloring:

If you want to decorate your handmade chocolates and make them have fun shapes and colors, you will need to use unique candy coloring because regular food coloring won't color the chocolate. It's necessary to have special food coloring that is made for candy and chocolate if you need the colors to show on the chocolate. You can find candy coloring at any craft supply store or candy supply store.

The tools above are some of the supplies you might need to make chocolate, but if you have these tools always on hand, you shouldn't have any trouble making delicious homemade chocolates. If you are going to make a special type of chocolate or use a special recipe, you might need specialized equipment. Still, in general, you can get your chocolate ready by just using these pieces of equipment and what you have in your kitchen.

CHAPTER 6

Making Sugar-Free Chocolate

If you're Diabetic on a diet where you can't tolerate sugar making, your sugar-free chocolate is an excellent way to enjoy a sweet treat without sugar. If you are making treats for a party or dinner and have friends or family attending, it would be great to include some sugar-free chocolates on the menu so that the people who can't have sugar or are watching their sugar intake could still have a nice treat.

There are different ways that you can make your sugar free chocolate. If you feel comfortable making your chocolate in your kitchen, you can use base chocolate like unsweetened chocolate with no sugar in it, but you'll have to add something to the chocolate to make it sweet. Add fruit juice to the unsweetened chocolate to sweeten it.

When you're mixing the sugar substitute with the unsweetened chocolate together, you should always mix them when they are dry, if not, they won't combine well, and they will separate when they are wet. Pour in little amounts of fruit juice to sweeten the unsweetened chocolate if you'll be using it, and make sure that you add a thickener to the chocolate. This will keep the right consistency of the chocolate.

You can always buy a diabetic-friendly or sugar-free chocolate in blocks or in chips from candy supply houses as a base for your choco treats if you don't feel comfy trying unsweetened chocolate base to sweeten it yourself. There is a high range of sugar-free chocolates, including milk and dark chocolate, in most candy supply houses. It's pretty good for anyone that can't have too much sugar.

You can make chocolate candy exactly like the regular chocolate by pouring it into the molds and letting it harden. Do this once you have unsweetened or sugar-free chocolate. If you want to make fancy chocolate treat like a chocolate dipping sauce for fresh fruit or chocolate mouse, you can still use the sugar-free chocolate as a base; then, you can try different recipes using the sugar-free chocolates as an ingredient.

Chop the small chips of the sugar free chocolate base if you want to make sugar free chocolate chip cookies, and adding them to some sugar free cookie dough. By the way, you'll need to be careful what temperature you bake the cookies at. If not, the chocolate will melt.

CHAPTER 7

Making Low-Free Chocolate

re you trying to lose weight? You might want to try making some low-fat chocolate you can keep around the house or maybe give to your friends who are trying to lose their weights. Homemade low-fat chocolates are well-known desserts for party favors at teen birthday favors or sleepover parties. It's pretty nice to have chocolates like these around when you want to enjoy some, so it's not necessarily thinking about how much fat is in the treats you're eating.

Looking for some pre-made low-fat chocolate chips or bricks that you can melt down and use to make your candies is a way to make some low-fat chocolates at home. You can also easily make your low-fat version of traditional chocolate that you can use to make cookies, brownies, or candy treats; if you don't want to spend too much money on a pricey pre-made chocolate base, you can't find low-fat chocolate that is pre-made. Another thing that makes a great low fat and

low-calorie dessert is the low-fat chocolate dipping sauce for fresh fruit, which won't make you feel like you're missing out on a treat.

Below are tips to make your low-fat Chocolate:

1)   Develop a taste for dark chocolate:
The dark Chocolate has the lowest fat content of the different kinds of chocolate, and it has no milk products in it.

2)   Substitute semisweet or bittersweet chocolate for milk chocolate:
The less cocoa butter or milk the chocolate has, the lower the fat will be.

3)   Don't add extras to your Chocolate:
You don't need to add anything to your chocolate, but you must add something, then make it some raisins that are healthier and lower in fat or chopped nuts that are good for your heart, then adding things like peanut butter chips or candy pieces.

4)   Use a chocolate coating instead of Chocolate:
Make a low-fat chocolate dipping sauce from some dark or semisweet chocolate and then lightly coat granola or some fresh fruit if you're craving for a sweet treat to keep your fat intake low. That way won't be eating a lot of fat in your chocolate.

5)   Making some low-fat hot chocolate instead of candy:
Use dark chocolate to make some low-fat hot chocolate and enjoy a hot chocolate cup instead of a high-fat dessert or candy.

The tips given above are some simple ways to still have chocolate treats without going overboard on your fat intake or worrying about ruining your diet. Suppose you're worried about how much fat your kids eat. In that case, you can just substitute some low-fat chocolate instead of normal chocolate in brownies, cookies, and chocolate milk can make a difference in how much fat the kiddos are eating every day.

CHAPTER 8

5 Fun Ways to Make Your Chocolate Unique

If you want to have fun making your homemade chocolate, you can play around with different ingredients and make your chocolate unique. Putting your brand logo/stamp/style on the chocolate will also make it more personal when you give it out as gifts to people you love.

And if someday you want to go further to sell your styled homemade chocolate prepared by you, then having your unique chocolates will make it a lot easier to sell.

But most people that make homemade chocolate use the same basic types of chocolate, and these chocolate are from candy supply stores.

So how can you make your unique chocolates without making it from scratch?

Below are five easy ways you can create delicious treats that reflect your style:

1.   Mix chocolate bases :
Just because most people who make homemade chocolate use the same bases don't mean that you can't make your base chocolate unique. You can use the same chocolate bases from candy supply stores, but you only have to combine them in a nice way to make your unique flavor.

Mixing dark chocolate and milk chocolate, or semisweet chocolate with white chocolate, or mixing other flavors to create your unique base can be a great way to make your homemade chocolates stand out from the crowd.

2.   Add things to your base chocolate :
There are lots of things that you can add to your chocolate base to make your chocolates taste good and more unique. You can use toasted sesame seeds to make your chocolate crunchy. You can also use peanut butter, seeds, nuts, fruits, and lots of things to make your chocolates different and delicious.

3.   Make your molds :
When it comes to putting your chocolates in a mold, you need to think outside the box to decide the kind of molds to use. Instead of using traditional candy molds in traditional shapes, you can use cake molds, soap molds, cookie cutters, and other tools to make unique shapes for your chocolates; it would be fun this way.

Are you interested in making your molds? You can find books and suppliers to make your plastic molds at most craft stores.

4.   Use unique packages :
How you package your chocolate candies matters a lot. You need to have a unique style of doing that. Your style should be different from other ways out there. Make it prettier than the commercial candies. You could package your candy so beautiful and fun by using a hand-painted box or little cello bags.

5.   Use decorations :

If you would like to decorate your chocolates, you can use candy coloring and other fun decorations, which will help turn the plainest homemade chocolate into a delightful treat. Make sure that you decorate your candy properly so the decorations won't fall off in the package.

CHAPTER 9

Using Molds

A great way to make your chocolate exciting and fun is by using molds. Use basic molds in traditional shapes like squares, molds in different styles and shapes. You can just make fun with it. *Are you looking towards making lollipops or suckers?* There are special molds that you can use to make them.

Many companies make special candy molds that are specifically made to be used with chocolate. These are mostly found in holiday shapes like Easter bunnies, chicks, eggs, or Christmas shapes like Santa Claus, stars, and Christmas trees. There are candy molds out there for every season, so you shouldn't have any trouble finding a mold that will be perfect for you during the holiday.

You can also find candy and craft molds at any craft store and sometimes at the grocery store. Some craft stores carry thin plastic

molds that are very cheap, but these don't last very long, so they're not a bargain. Spend a few dollars more and get molds made from high-density plastic that are very thick. They're worth the extra cost.

You are not limited to just using candy molds for your chocolate. You can use soap molds, cake molds, or other types of molds too. As long as mold is made from heavy plastic, then it should work just fine.

To make your candy, spray the inside of the mold using a non-stick cooking spray. This way, you won't have a problem where half of your chocolate candy ends up stuck inside the mold. If chocolate does get stuck inside a mold turn, then mold over so that the open side is facing down. The next thing you'll want to do is place the mold under running water from the tap until the chocolate loosens and slides out.

To take care of your molds, make sure that you wash each of the molds thoroughly after doing it. Molds can be washed with normal soap and water like dishes.

When you pour the chocolate into the molds, it might take several hours or even several days for the chocolate to harden in the mold. Even though you might be tempted to put the chocolate and the mold into the freezer so that it hardens more quickly - you shouldn't do that.

It will make the chocolate harden too fast, and it can damage the mold. You can put the chocolate-filled mold in the refrigerator, though, which should help the chocolate solidify in the mold more quickly.

CHAPTER 10

Tips for Making Better Homemade Chocolate

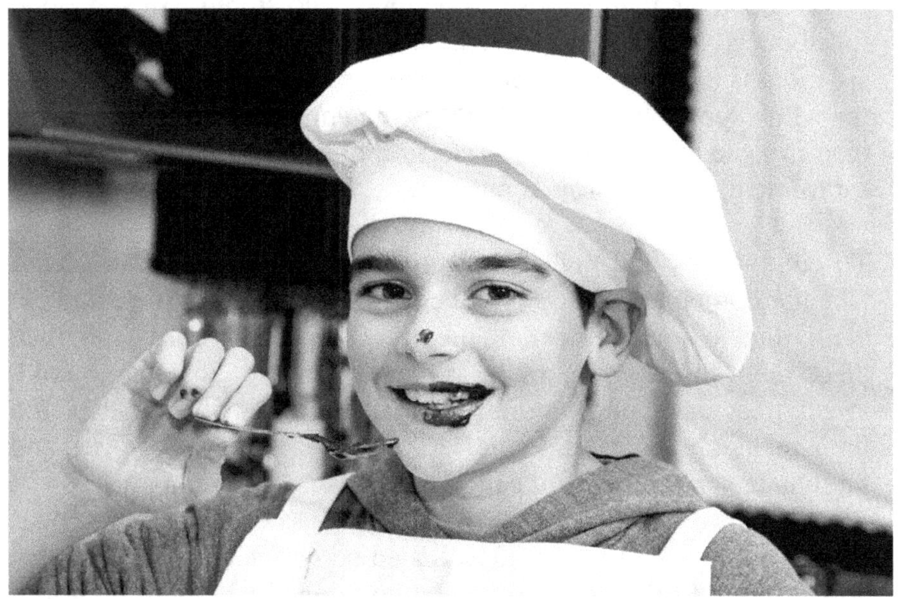

Everyone has their preferred methods of making homemade chocolates, and the fact is 'making some homemade chocolates is the only way you can learn' This chapter is packed with quick tips that you can use to make your homemade chocolate better.

- When you buy wafers or chips of chocolates that you're going to melt like a chocolate base for your candy, make sure you don't take them out of their plastic bags. Use a double boiler them and then cut a small hole in the corner of the bag; then use the bag to pour the chocolate into molds.

- After microwaving the chocolate, melt for about a minute and keep microwaving it until it's melted, for another minute. Every microwave is different, and each type of chocolate has a different melting point, so the time needed to melt the chocolate will be

different on every microwave. You have to melt the chocolate for one minute so you won't accidentally burn the chocolate.

- Don't freeze your chocolate concoctions. Freezing will start to make the chocolate break down, and you'll lose the delicious flavor of homemade chocolate. Instead of freezing the chocolate, store it in an airtight container at room temperature.

- Dark Chocolate that is properly wrapped and stored will stay good for about a year, but milk chocolate will only stay good for just six months. If it's getting longer than six months, you should look for white spots on the chocolate. If the chocolate has white spots, then it means the chocolate is starting to separate, and you should eat immediately or throw it out.

- To cut calories and make your homemade chocolate last longer, take the homemade candy or chocolate bars that you made and cut them into a bunch of small pieces. Wrap the pieces, and then place them in the refrigerator. When you or the kids want a cold, sweet treat on a hot summer day, take out a piece of the cold homemade chocolate and enjoy it. It will have fewer calories and fat than ice cream or a full candy bar and taste delicious.

- If you're really in a jam and you need some chocolate to eat, and you're out of chocolate, and maybe you don't have the time to run to the candy supply store or craft store to get more, or if the craft and hobby stores near you don't carry candy making chocolate, you can get some melted chocolate chips. It isn't a great solution, but it's a solution when you need some emergency chocolate for a recipe.

- If your Chocolate does develop white spots and you are not going to eat it right away, but don't want to throw it out, you can just melt the chocolate down, add some new ingredients, put it in new molds, and then wrap it, and keep for later.

CHAPTER 11

Tips for Packaging Your Homemade Chocolate

There is much fun when it comes to packaging your homemade chocolate treats, which you can give as a gift for special occasions or just as a treat for your family and friends. We have several ways to package your chocolates, but one thing you need to have in mind is that you must store your chocolate in an airtight container if it's not going to be eaten immediately.

You should always keep the chocolate fresh. Homemade chocolate usually comes wrapped in two wrappers. One that is decorative, and the other is airtight. You can go for a traditional gold-colored candy box with pillow sheets inserted. The sheets' color should be the same as the candy boxes. These are popular and great during Christmas and Valentine. So it will really help in packaging your chocolates.

Using cello craft bags is another idea as well. They are easy to use and are not expensive. Mostly, they come in different colors or prints, so they are great for wrapping homemade chocolates on birthdays. You can get your cello bags at any craft supply or candy supply store. Also, get them online in bulk, and get great discounts if you're using many cello bags.

Cello bags are the best for packaging if you're making suckers or lollipops. They won't stick to the chocolate as the plastic wrap will. Firstly, put a cello bag over the top of the sucker, then heat the cello bag using an air dryer, and the bag will mold to the shape of the candy without sticking to it. You make the chocolate look cute and fresh; you can put a sticker or ribbon.

The finishing touch is so important in your packaging. Whatever packaging you pick for your homemade chocolate, make sure it's unique, and it should reflect your personality and make a good impression. You might think it's unnecessary to spend a lot of money or time packaging your chocolate, but it is really worth taking that last step of packaging your chocolate.

Most importantly, your homemade chocolate's creative packaging doesn't have to be expensive to be great but needs to be something you can put your artistic stamp on - designing it yourself.

CHAPTER 12

Homemade Chocolate Ideas for Christmas

Surprise your families and friends during the holidays with this homemade chocolates. Have a great time with them during the Christmas, and make sure you share these inexpensive chocolates and make them feel great.

Below are ideas that you can use to make your Christmas holiday more festive with homemade chocolate:

- Homemade chocolates wrapped in plastic and arranged in a pretty holiday container make wonderful and inexpensive gifts for teachers, ministers, postal carriers, newspaper carriers, delivery people, bosses, Secret Santa gift exchanges, and holiday parties.

- Make some homemade chocolates and serve them with fresh fruits when you need to bring a dessert to a holiday party.

- These chocolates are great stocking stuffers.

- Make a rich holiday by enjoying this homemade chocolate on a cold winter night.

- Do you need gifts for many people, like kids in your child's class at school, colleagues in colleges, co-workers in your office? In a small candy box, place one or two homemade chocolates and decorate the outside for the box with markers, paint, and glue, then you have a unique gift that does not take lots of time to make or cost a lot.

- During the holiday, cut out some of the homemade chocolate a cookie-cutter.

- Make low fat and sugar-free homemade chocolates instead of a Christmas cookie to keep the number of calories you consume the holidays under control.

- Make some homemade chocolate cherry bark or chocolate bark and arrange it on a platter with some fresh fruit. Then you can use that as an edible centerpiece for your table.

CHAPTER 13

Make the Holidays More Festive with Homemade Chocolate Drinks

During the winter holidays, you will see lots of people craving for hot chocolate drinks. Almost everyone loves it! This is the kind of drink you can share with people at parties. Homemade hot chocolate can also be given to kids as gifts. It's free from alcohol, so you can share it where kids are present.

Instead of spending a lot of money on fancy hot chocolate mixes this year's holiday, why not make your own unique hot chocolate mixes and serve as gifts or keep in the pantry for family and friends. It would save you a whole lot of money.

The first thing you need to make this homemade hot chocolate is 'cocoa powder.' You can buy unsweetened or sweetened cocoa powder in any grocery store; it's usually in the aisle where the syrups and

chocolate milk powders are kept. It's so easy to prepare this Homemade hot chocolate mixes.

Then you need some powdered milk or powdered non-dairy creamer. If you want to make your homemade hot chocolate very rich, then creamer is the one you should go for. Most experts suggest that you use powdered milk, but add a touch of powdered creamer to make it rich. Enhance the flavor of the hot cocoa using a flavored non-dairy creamer.

You can use your cooking skills and imagination to put together some exotic hot cocoa mix treat once you have cocoa powder, creamer base, and milk.

Some ideas that you can use to prepare your tasty hot chocolate this holiday season are given below:

- Use unsweetened cocoa or use a sugar substitute to sweeten the cocoa powder for diabetic people or people that can't have sugar.
- Add spices and herbs to make Mexican hot chocolate or other hot and spicy hot chocolate types.
- Add dried fruit and herbs to kick your hot chocolate.
- To make a hot chocolate mix that everyone will love, add mini marshmallows.
- Combine different types of cocoa powder to get different flavors.
- To make low-fat hot chocolate mix, use dark cocoa powder and low-fat creamer and milk.
- To make a very personal gift on a budget, make up several different kinds of hot chocolate mixes and package them in plastic bags inside pretty envelopes and pack them in a basket with two mugs and some homemade chocolates or cookies - *so lovely!*
- When you're packaging your hot chocolate, it's good to list all the package ingredients. It's necessary because you might have given someone who is allergic to one of the ingredients.

CHAPTER 14

Homemade Chocolate Ideas for Easter

There's no Easter celebration that would be complete without lots of chocolate, and every chocolate love gets excited around Easter. Save your money during this Easter holiday and make your homemade chocolate treats for Easter.

Since nearly everyone goes overboard and eats too much chocolate during the Easter holiday, it's good to make a low calorie, low fat, or sugar-free Chocolate during Easter. That way, you can eat the same amount of candy, but you'll be eating fewer calories and less fat, and so will your kids.

Here are some ideas that you can use to make your homemade chocolates for Easter:

- Put your twist on classic chocolate bunnies using exotic chocolates or an unusual chocolate base like chocolate mixed with spices or fruit to make chocolate bunnies.
- Make edible homemade chocolate baskets instead of chocolate bunnies, then arrange other holiday treats inside the basket. To make a chocolate Easter basket, melt some base chocolate in a plastic bag and blow up a small balloon. Put the balloon inside the bag of melted chocolate until the balloon's bottom half is thickly coated with chocolate and immediately move the balloon to the refrigerator.
- Once the Chocolate hardens, pop the balloon and pull the balloon out, and you'll have a solid chocolate Easter basket that you can use for your kids or as a holiday table centerpiece. You can even use white chocolate as a base and dye it with food coloring to make your chocolate baskets in different colors. Be careful, though! The chocolate might melt if left out in the warm weather.
- If you want to cut down on the amount of sugar that your kids will be eating during the Easter holiday, make a chocolate dipping sauce and then cut fruit into Easter shapes and dip the fruit into the chocolate. Once the chocolate hardens, your kids will have a sweet holiday treat with a lot less sugar and calories. I hope they enjoy it!
- Make some dark chocolate eggs and use candy coloring to paint the chocolate eggs. Do this instead of decorating hard-boiled eggs in pretty colors.
- Most Easter candies are made from milk chocolate, so stay away from using milk chocolate in your homemade Easter candy bases and use something more exotic to make your homemade chocolate stand out more. *Enjoy!*

CHAPTER 15

Homemade Chocolate Ideas for Other Holidays

You can make many great gifts, party favors, centerpieces, and other for other holidays. Below are some fun ways to use homemade chocolates for other holidays:

■ **For Valentine's Day:**

Nothing says "I love you" than some homemade chocolates on Valentine's Day. Since the price of candy and flowers usually goes sky high around Valentine's Day, making your homemade chocolates for your sweetheart can be a great way to save money and still give that special person a gift that he/she will love. **When you need a special homemade valentine treat, you can:**

- Make homemade chocolates using some "naughty" chocolate molds for a little bit of fun.
- Plan a sensuous dessert by cutting up some fresh fruit and making an exotic, spicy chocolate dipping sauce.
- Make your sweetie a dozen chocolate rose lollipops instead of giving a dozen roses.
- Use Valentine-themed cookie cutters to make special chocolate bars and fudge pieces.
- Make homemade chocolates that your kids can bring to school and share with classmates instead of buying expensive valentines.
- Surprise your sweetie with heart-shaped pancakes and homemade chocolate sauce for breakfast.
- Make some special hot chocolate mixes as gifts for friends and family.
- Mix up an exotic chocolate sauce and serve it warm over some ice cream.
- Have an Anti- Valentine's Day party and make some dark chocolate broken heart candies for your single friends.
- Make homemade chocolate gift bags for everyone in the office.
- Use Valentine's Day molds to create chocolate Cupids and then decorate them with candy coloring. Give one to everyone you meet on Valentine's Day.
- Make yourself a special Valentine's Day chocolate treat and fill some dark chocolate truffles with champagne and a little rosewater.
- Make a box of homemade chocolates for your partner and top each one with a rose petal.

■ For Mother's Day:

Mother's Day is another holiday that you can make a lot more special by giving homemade chocolate. Remember, your mom loved the presents you made with your own hands the best when you were younger.

Moms always love handmade presents the best, so this year, make her some delicious homemade chocolate treats. The only limit to making homemade chocolate gifts is your imagination, but here are some ideas to get you started:

- Use a mother and child's soap mold to make some special Mother's Day chocolates in a cameo. Ensure that you use a chocolate base made up of mom's favorite types of chocolate.
- Make a gift basket for mom with homemade chocolates, special hot chocolate mixes, new mugs, and a soothing CD to play when she needs to relax.
- Make coupons that promise your mother homemade chocolate treat every month and a visit from you.
- Sit, relax, and share a cup of tea and some homemade chocolate with your mom.

- Make a sauce of mom's favorite chocolate and drizzle it over some buttered popcorn to make chocolate popcorn balls. Mom will love to have a crunchy, sweet snack to enjoy when she's watching TV.
- If you have small children, making homemade chocolate is a fantastic way for the kids to make something to give to their mom, but always supervise them when they're around the hot liquid chocolate.
- Have your kids decorate gift boxes with glitter and crayons and pack the boxes full of homemade chocolates.
- Have each child make a handprint in chocolate for mom.
- Give your mom the best gift you can give her the gift of your time. Spend the afternoon in the kitchen with your mom making homemade chocolate together and eating everything that you make.
- Handmade gifts mean more to mothers than anyone else, and making some homemade chocolate as a gift would be great, let it be a gift she'll always remember, so this year, instead of buying her another, taking her to a fancy brunch that is crowded and overpriced, you can just make her some homemade chocolate and watch her face light up.

CHAPTER 16

Homemade Chocolate Ideas for Birthdays

It's pretty amazing making and sharing homemade chocolates at birthday parties. They go hand in hand. There are different ways you can use homemade chocolate at birthday parties. Homemade chocolate is always a big hit, most especially at kid's birthday parties.

Below are fun ways in which you can use homemade chocolate to liven up birthday parties.

- **Making homemade chocolate lollipops for your kid's birthday party:** Chocolate suckers and lollipops are great party favors because they can be wrapped individually. They are so easy to carry around. Even if your child's birthday party location is in a museum park or restaurant, you can easily hand out homemade suckers as party favors.

- **Making sugar-free homemade chocolates in shapes that goes in line with the party's theme:** Get a small Chinese food take out boxes; you can get them in bulk online if you want. Bring out stickers, crayons, glue, glitter, and other materials, then give the kids the chance to decorate their party favor box - it's always fun to them. Then place homemade sugar-free chocolate in the boxes when the kids are leaving. Other parents will appreciate that their kids can have a sweet and sugar-free treat to take home.
- **Making chocolate boxes for the kids to put their other party items into and take home:** Chocolate boxes are always a hit at birthday parties.
- You can make one the party activities to be 'making their chocolate (only if the kids are old enough). Assist them in melting the chocolate in the microwave, then giving them the chance to add their fun style and items into the chocolate like fruits, candy, nuts, etc. Let them choose a mold and pour their chocolate concoction in it. The chocolates should be heard and ready to take home before the party is over.
- For grownup parties, you can set up a chocolate fountain flowing with some delicious homemade chocolate sauce. For dipping, set up a fruit bar full of fresh fruits. This will give people that ca concern about their calorie intake a low-calorie dessert alternative.
- Also, use homemade chocolates as prizes for some of the party games. Each winner chooses their gift bag full of delicious chocolates.
- Give out a mug at grownup parties with a decorated packet of the special hot chocolate mix inside. Then you can print the recipe on any of the items so your guests can make it when they are free.
- It's always nice to serve something chocolatey at birthday parties.
- If you don't care about the chocolate, you can make your guest happy by serving some homemade chocolate. Let them have some chocolates to enjoy.

CHAPTER 17

Homemade Chocolate Ideas for Weddings & Wedding Showers

*H*ave you ever thought of using homemade chocolates for weddings and wedding shower? Do you know that homemade chocolates fit in perfectly for weddings and wedding showers?

Well, you're lucky to have found this content. Homemade wedding favors are an excellent way for the bride and groom to save some money. This is because it cost a lot less than the commercial ones.

You could share these favors to your friends and families to thank them for coming to celebrate the wedding with you. Since homemade chocolates are a personal gift, they are a perfect "thank you" message for family and friends.

There are several ways to incorporate homemade chocolates into your wedding, and below are a few ways people use homemade chocolates at weddings.

- Get some nice glasses, like a champagne glass, and fill them with homemade chocolates, wrapped.
- Over the top, place a square of tulle, then use a ribbon to tie the tulle down, so the chocolate won't fall out. Place one at each guest's seat.
- Chocolate boxes are made in the shape of a heart with the bride and groom's names. You can make it more personal by carving each guest's name into the chocolate box to make sure that you give the right box to the honorable guest! Then, you're' good.
- Bottles of chocolate dipping sauce labeled with the bride and groom's name, dates, and a kitschy name are fun wedding favors.
- Give your guests packets of special hot chocolate and two mugs in a basket with a book of love poems and instructions to sit and read the book together over a special homemade hot chocolate cup.
- Make a centerpiece of homemade chocolate roses on sticks decorated to look like stems and have each guest take one of the chocolate roses home with them at the end of the night.
- In the kid's area, set up a station where kids can make their chocolate to keep them occupied. Just make sure that they are supervised and that aprons are available to protect their nice clothes.
- Have a chocolate fountain flowing with a unique "signature" chocolate flavor and have plenty of strawberries and other fresh fruit available for dipping.
- A great wedding favor is to package a few homemade chocolates with a small, handwritten recipe book full of great recipes for homemade chocolates. Give the recipes fun names like **"Spice up your marriage Spicy Hot Chocolate."**

Homemade Chocolate Ideas for Other Occasions

You don't need a holiday or a wedding or a birthday as an excuse to make some homemade chocolate. Homemade chocolates are always a treat, and almost any party or gathering is more fun with some homemade chocolate.

If you are looking for an activity to keep the kids busy on a rainy afternoon, or a project that you can achieve together with your kids, or something special that you can make for a friend on a limited budget, spending a little time and a little money-making homemade chocolate can brighten your day, or your someone else's.

Below are some inexpensive and easy ways that you can use homemade chocolates to brighten someone's day:

- If you have been very busy lately and haven't had a lot of time left over to do things with your kids, you can make a date to spend just an hour in the evening making homemade chocolates with them. The process of making chocolate is easy and fun, and it will give you a chance to reconnect with your kids.
- Make some homemade chocolates in heart shapes after your spouse goes to bed and leave a small box of homemade candy tied with a red ribbon on his/her pillow the next morning - that's so sweet!
- Surprise a co-worker who has difficulty adjusting to something at work with a "pick me up" gift box of homemade chocolates and some special tea and a mug.
- Leave some special homemade hot chocolate mixes in the break room at work so that everyone can enjoy a nice sweet treat in the afternoon.
- Send a small box of homemade chocolates in fun shapes to school with your kids for their teachers as a small "thank you" gift for no reason.
- Suppose any of your friends have a bad breakup or have relationship problems. In that case, you can leave a gift basket on her doorstep with some homemade chocolates, a DVD of her favorite movie, some wine, and new silk pajamas or a cozy bathrobe and slippers.
- Put some small, personal wrapped pieces of homemade chocolate in your child's jacket pocket at random times.
- When you leave a tip for the waiter at your favorite restaurant or the barista that makes your coffee, you can leave a few personal wrapped homemade chocolates too.
- Bring over some homemade hot chocolate and two mugs to a lonely neighbor, then sit down, talk, and share the hot chocolate.

CHAPTER 19

Making Gourmet Homemade Chocolate

Most times, when people think about making homemade chocolate, they think about someone. So working in the kitchen and making some tasty chocolate would be great, but not the kind of high-end chocolate you find in a gourmet store. But you can make some gourmet chocolate at home, which doesn't have to cost a fortune to make.

Suppose you have a very sophisticated palette, and you enjoy gourmet chocolate but don't like paying $7 or more for a gourmet chocolate bar. In that case, you can easily make your gourmet chocolate at home.

The ingredients make the chocolate. So whenever you're cooking or baking, the quality of the ingredients you use to make a difference. You can taste the difference if you bake cookies with butter instead of margarine. Instead of imitation vanilla, you can use real vanilla extract;

it tastes different as well. The same principle applies when you're making gourmet chocolate at home. If you want to make the kind of chocolate that your friends and family will swear you bought from a gourmet shop, then using only high-quality ingredients is the best.

If you want to make gourmet chocolate, you can buy melt and styled chocolate bases made from higher-end ingredients, instead of placing an order for cacao beans, then grinding, roasting, and going through the entire traditional candy-making process.

Get your high-end gourmet chocolate, making materials online. There are several retailers you can get them from. Place an order for high-quality melt and pout style chocolate. Get extra important ingredients to use as add-ins in your gourmet chocolate.

Hit up your local farmer's grocery or store to get the best organic ingredients at a reasonable price - this is a tricky way to save money on your add-ins. Buy organic nuts, and make your peanut butter blends; you can also get luxury sugars, syrups, oil, and fresh herbs like rosehips and lavender to add into your gourmet chocolate.

Add in different kinds of high-end alcohol to some of your chocolate when you're making your gourmet chocolate. This will give it a great exotic taste. You could pair flavored raspberry vodka with some high-quality dark chocolate base and a few dried raspberries to make a wonderfully sweet and dark homemade chocolate.

Making gourmet chocolate might take more practice than making regular homemade chocolate because the flavors in gourmet chocolate need to be very subtle. Still, if you love gourmet chocolate, you can learn to make it at home and have a lot of fun making your gourmet chocolate flavors.

CHAPTER 20

Make Money Selling Homemade Chocolate

Have you discovered that you have a real passion for making *homemade chocolate already?* Once you realized you're putting a smile on people's faces, your friends and families can't stop saying nice things about your homemade chocolate making.

Then you might want to try to make a little extra money if you're genuinely passionate about making homemade chocolate. You could try selling yours and making some extra money.

Firstly, if you're ready to start selling your homemade chocolate, do research about your state/country's licensing requirements to have a commercial kitchen. You need to either rent a kitchen that has been inspected or have your kitchen checked. Be ready to start making your homemade chocolate as soon as you have a certificate saying that your

kitchen is approved. Also, when you have all the necessary paperwork to start selling homemade chocolate, then you can go ahead.

The next thing is you need to find out what your niche market is. Who are you trying to sell homemade chocolates to? Are you going to make homemade chocolates wedding favors or other party favors ? or do you want to make as many types of homemade chocolates as you can?

Sometimes people get started selling their homemade chocolates by selling them at churches, craft fairs, museums, beaches, and other places known to your target market. You can start selling from small by getting your family and friends to buy your homemade chocolate.

It would be great if you can have a sit, map out a basic business plan, and set some goals for your business. Even if you want to sell these chocolates as part-time, you still need to set your goals and have a business plan.

You can set up a website where people can order homemade chocolates from you once you're ready to take orders. Do personal research into different shipping methods available, and how much each one cost because each freight carrier will have their terms and conditions about shipping food. You can also want to sell wholesale to bakeries and local stores; you don't need to bother shipping food hassles. Your local gourmet stores or food company might be interested in buying your homemade chocolates. Most of them would want to buy them in bulk and sometimes accept consignment sales by paying them a percentage of your earnings.

Likewise, you might think about offering your homemade chocolate recipe books for sale or starting a blog for homemade chocolate making if you love making chocolates, and you have developed your unique and special recipes. *Are you looking towards putting a lot of time and effort into making your business grow?* Homemade chocolate making can help in making extra money and can be a great hobby as well.

CHAPTER 21

Conclusion

I hope you've gained a lot about making your chocolate at home through this book. It's exciting making chocolates at home, and as a hobby, which happens to be an amazing way to show your friends and families how much you mean to them. Nothing tells someone you love them like giving them an edible gift like homemade chocolate. Of course, they would appreciate it.

Likewise, making homemade chocolate can save you extra money on gifts. Holiday gifts, Birthday gifts, Anniversary gifts, and other gifts can be quite pricey. If you have many friends and family, you probably almost always have to get a gift for someone. So making homemade chocolate can be less expensive than buying gifts. This gives a chance to make something different.

When making homemade chocolates, you can invite your kids as well. You know it's a great way to connect with them. Parents who work and are very busy mostly don't get to spend a lot of quality time with their kids. Therefore, making some homemade chocolate together can be a nice chance to connect with your kids.

You might want to open your own mini business making homemade chocolate if you love cooking and making chocolates. Being creative and getting several ways to make homemade chocolate will surely be the keys to your success. The tips and ideas in this book should assist you in getting started on that journey.

I wish you Goodluck as you dive into the exciting world of making homemade chocolate. *Enjoy!*

www.ingramcontent.com/pod-product-compliance
Lightning Source LLC
Chambersburg PA
CBHW081407130726
47998CB00011B/3105